Pursuing PERFECT HAND DRAWN ANIMALS

a How to Activity Book

ACTIVIBOOKS FOR KIDS

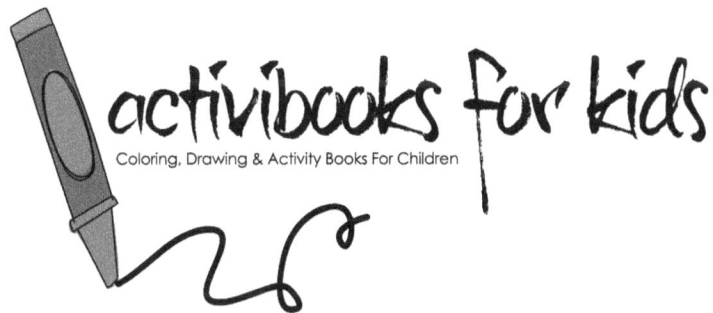

activibooks for kids
Coloring, Drawing & Activity Books For Children

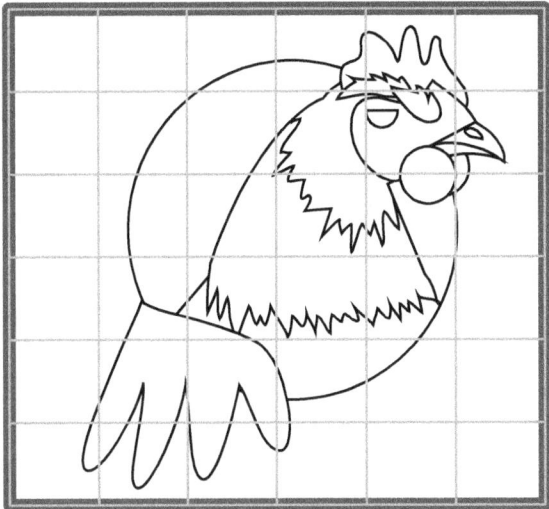

DRAW
THE
IMAGE

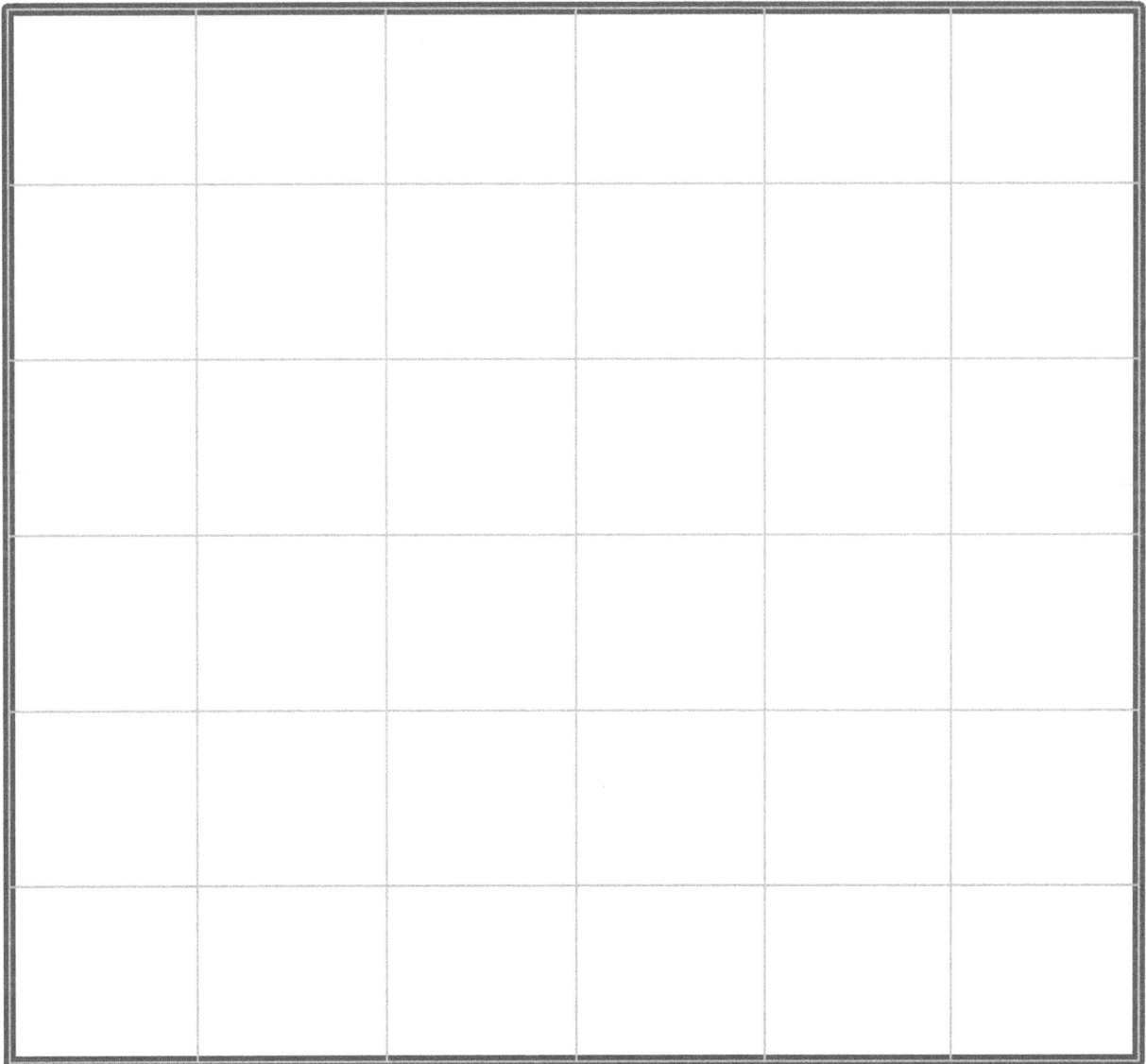

DRAW
THE
IMAGE

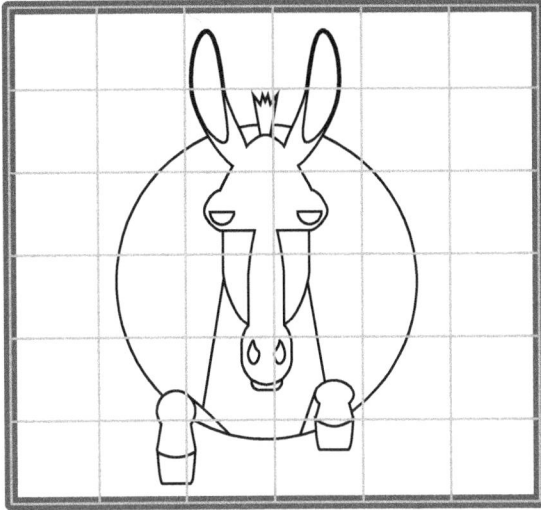

DRAW
THE
IMAGE

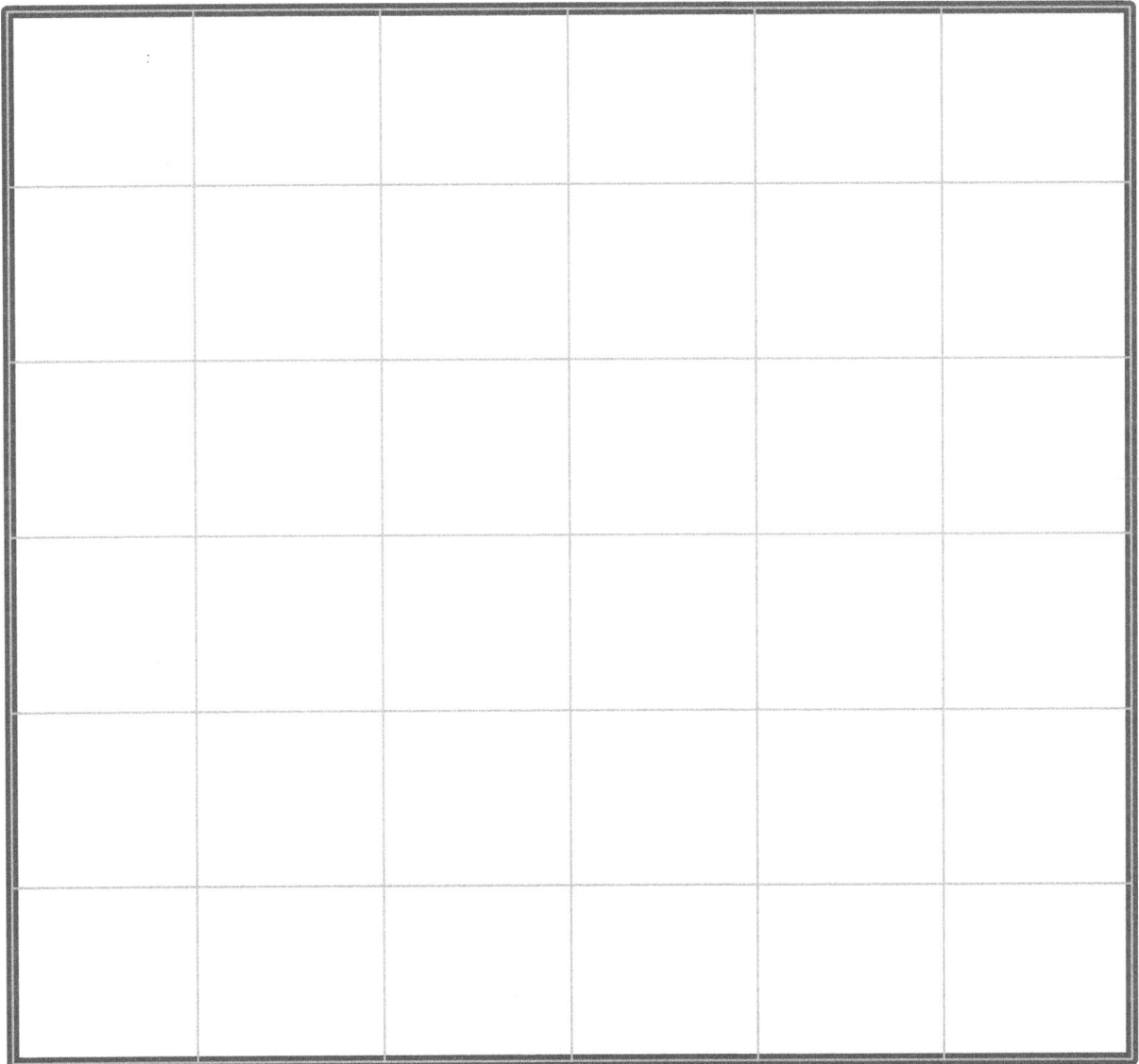

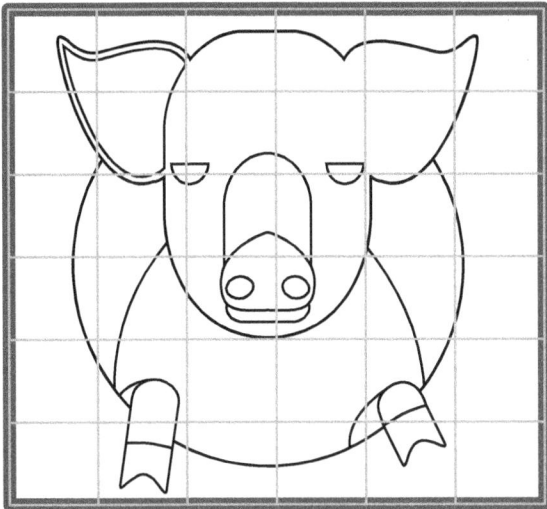

DRAW
THE
IMAGE

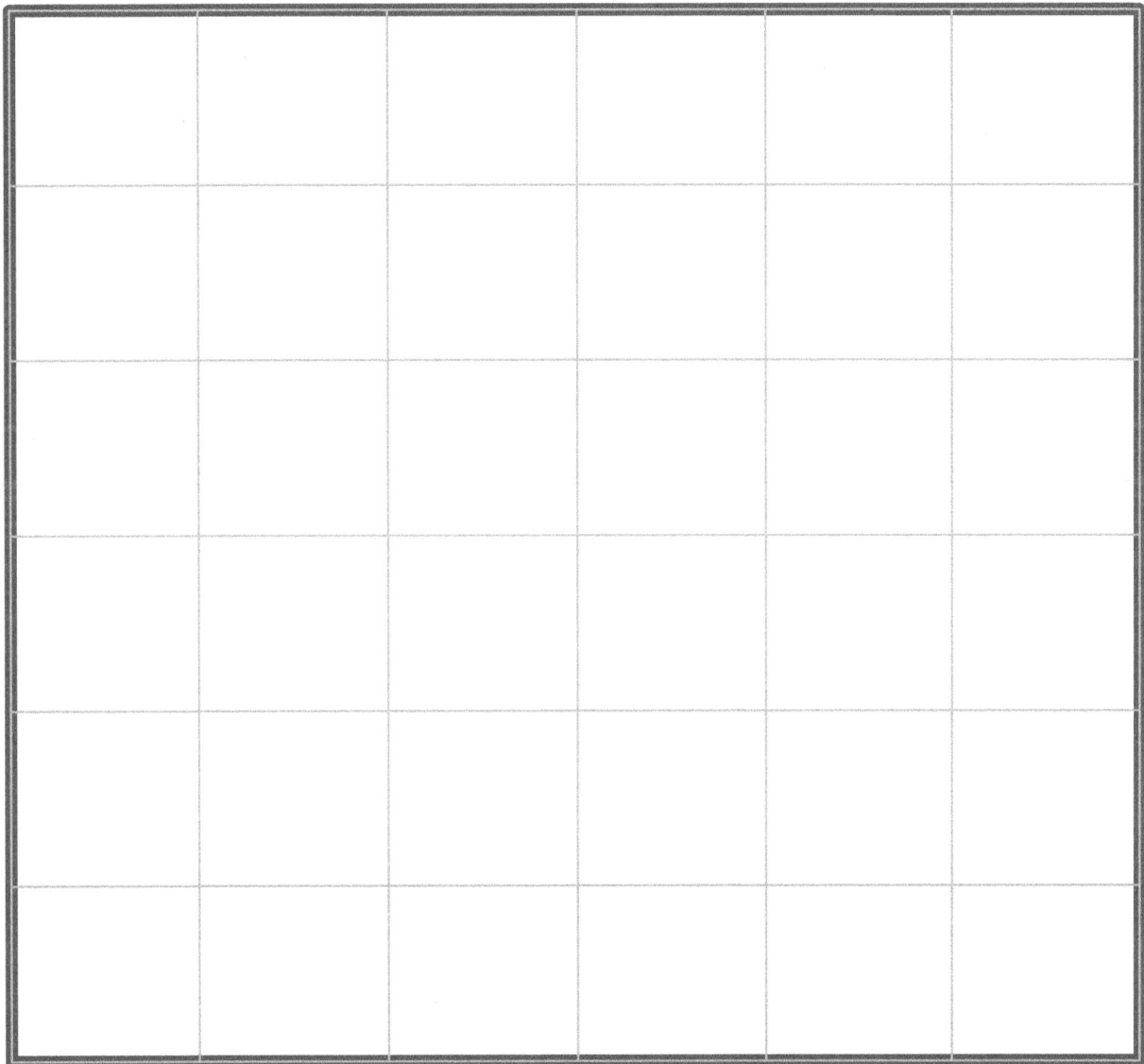

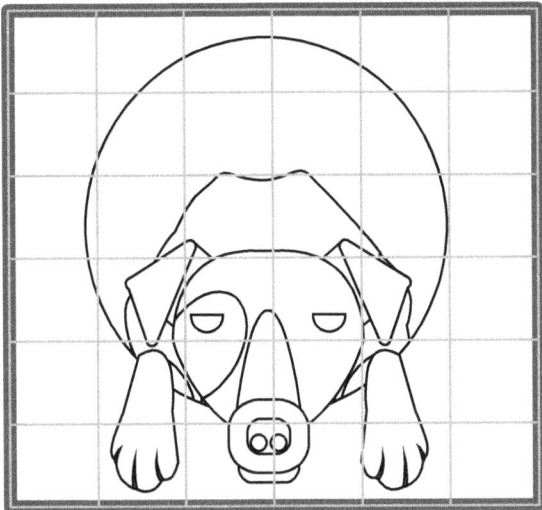

DRAW
THE
IMAGE

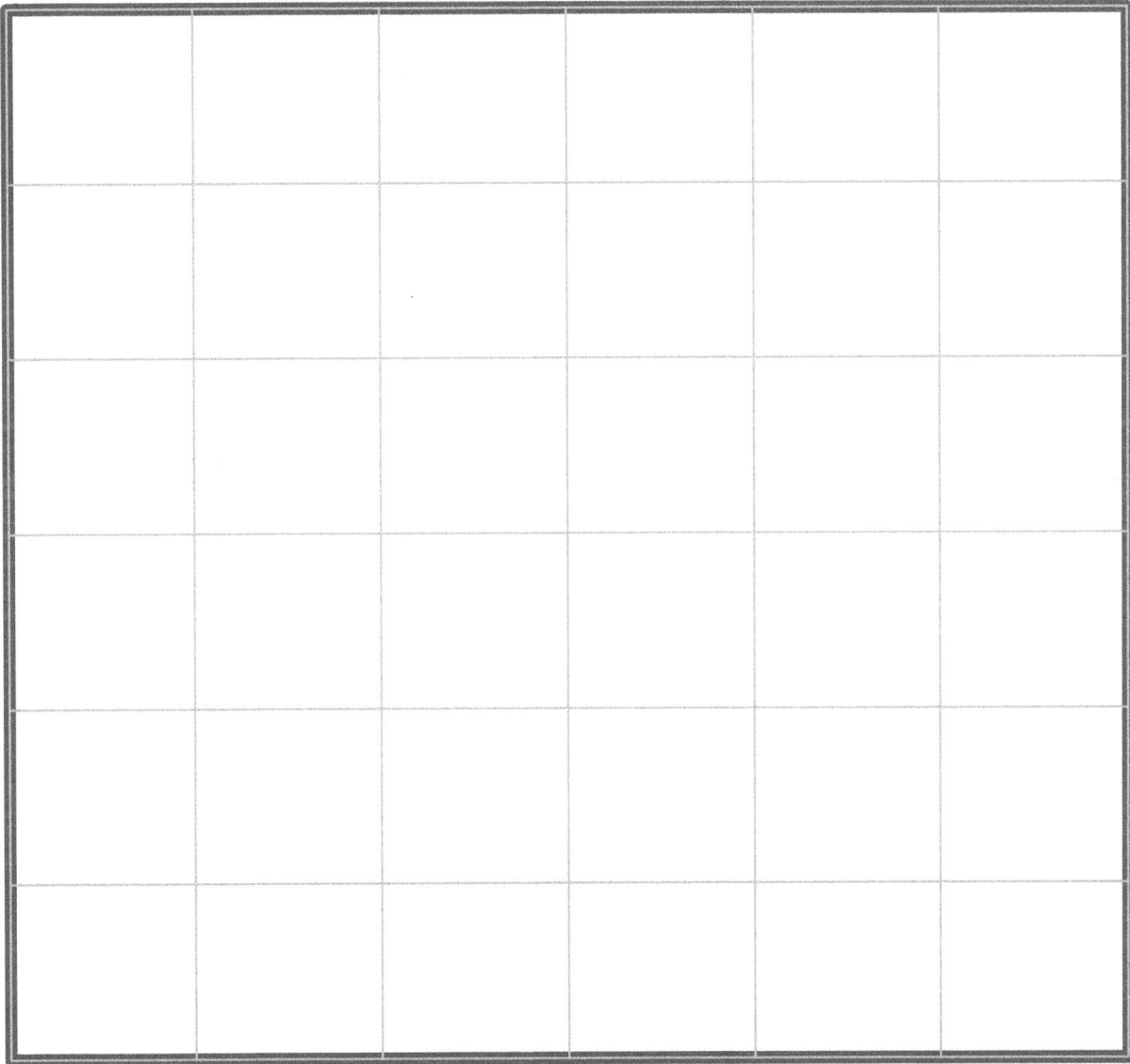

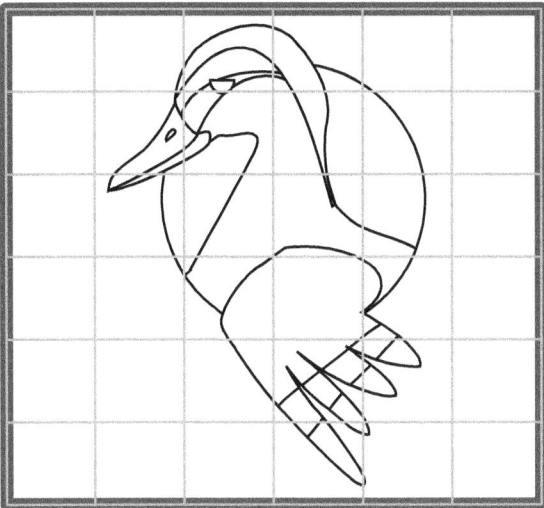

DRAW
THE
IMAGE

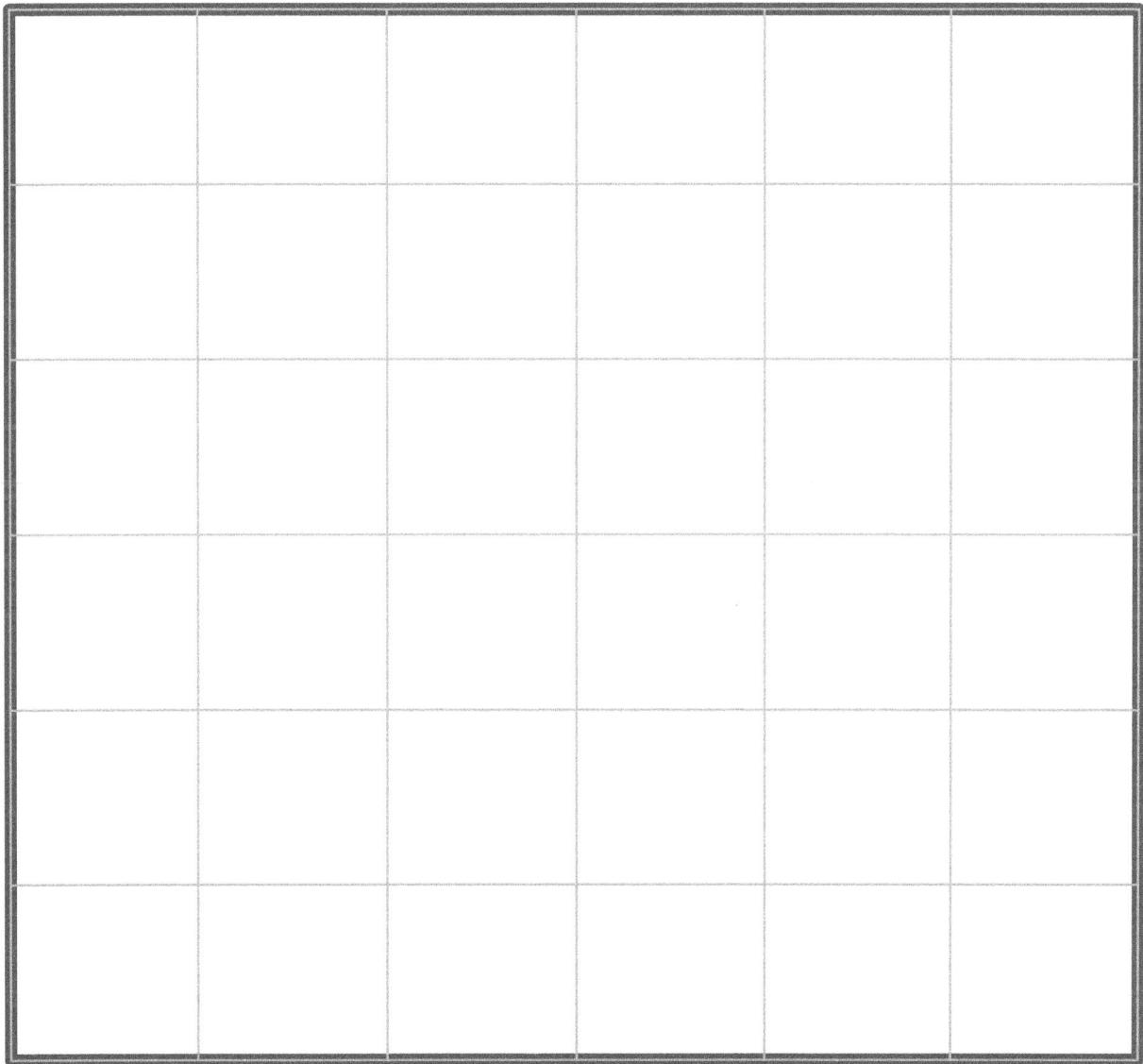

DRAW
THE
IMAGE

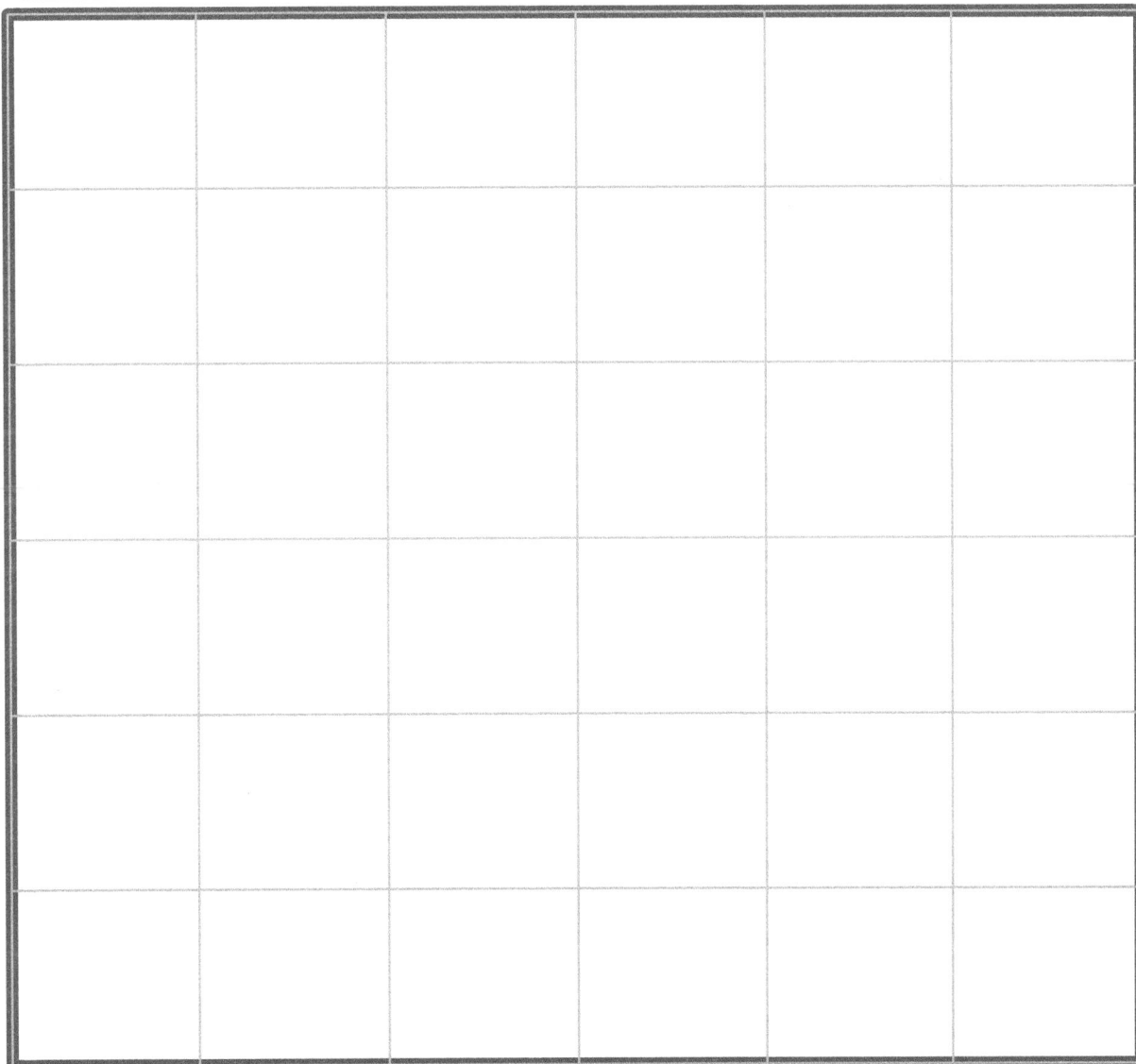

DRAW
THE
IMAGE

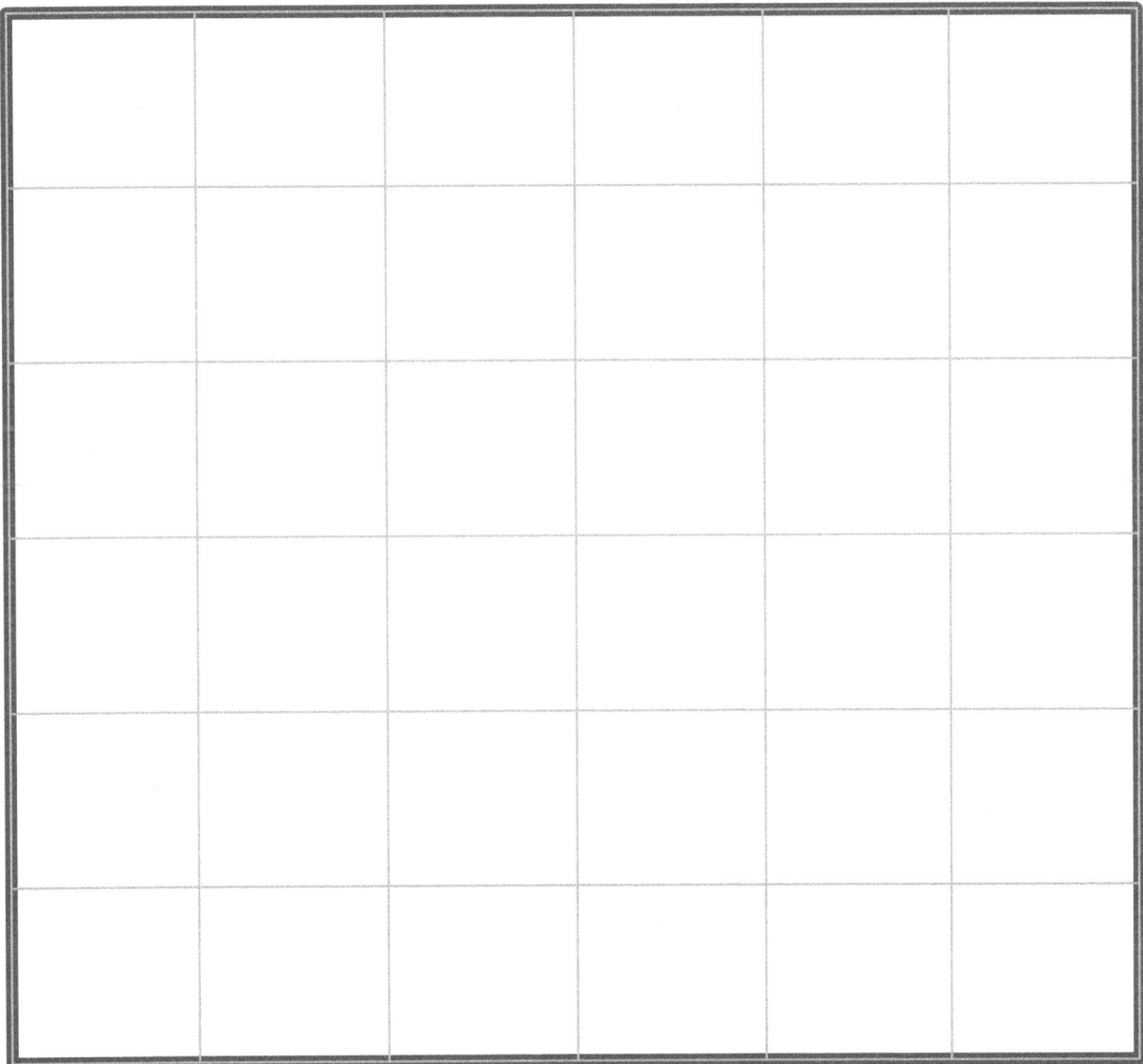

DRAW
THE
IMAGE

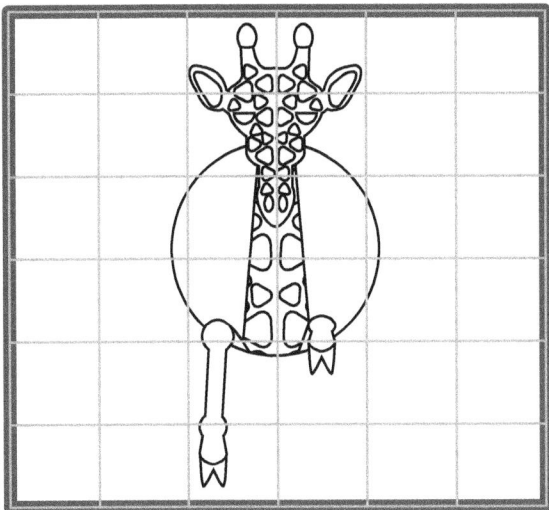

DRAW
THE
IMAGE

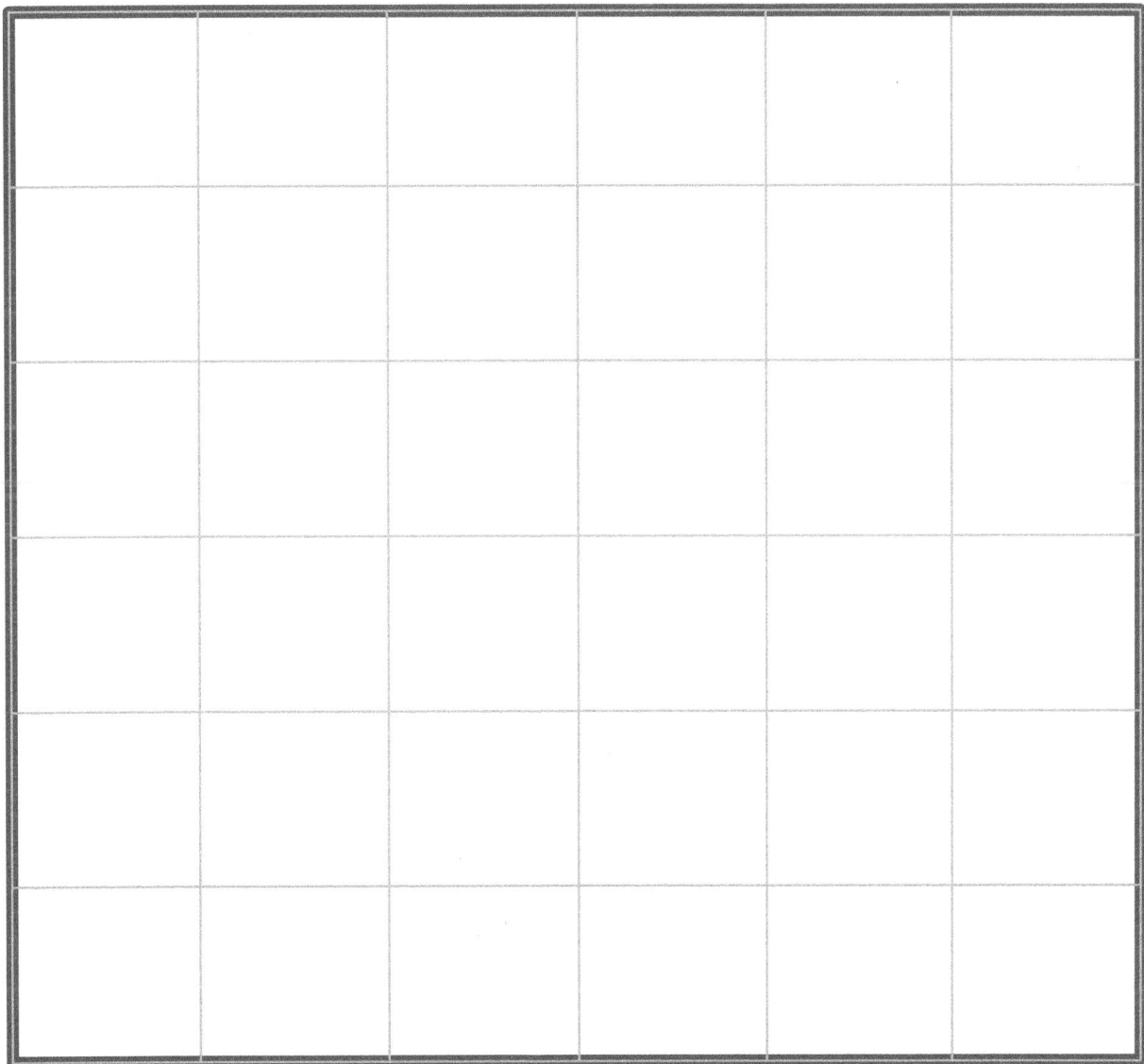

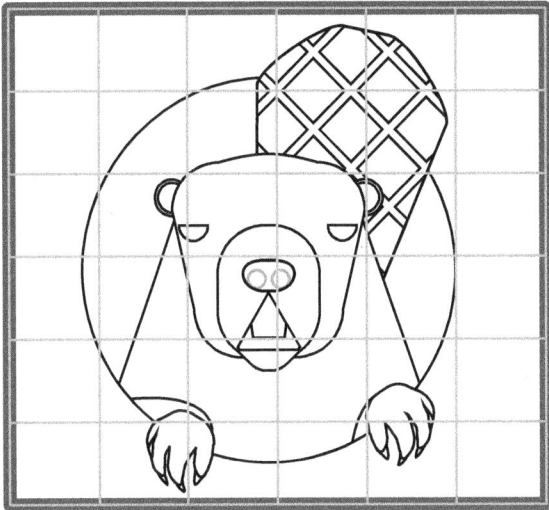

DRAW
THE
IMAGE

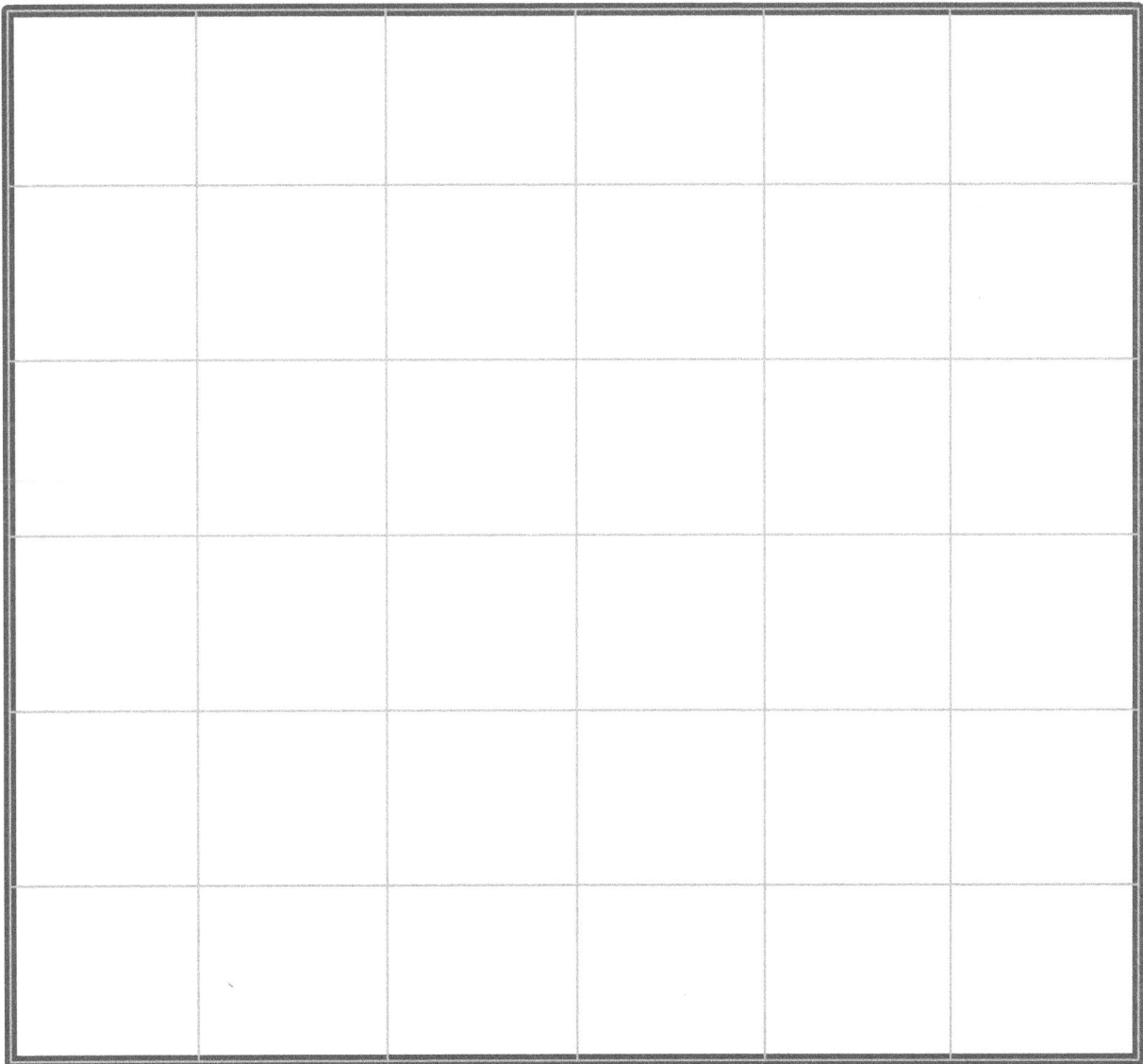

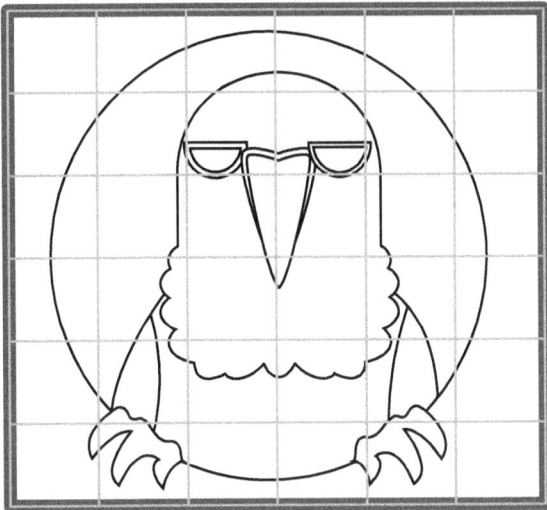

DRAW
THE
IMAGE

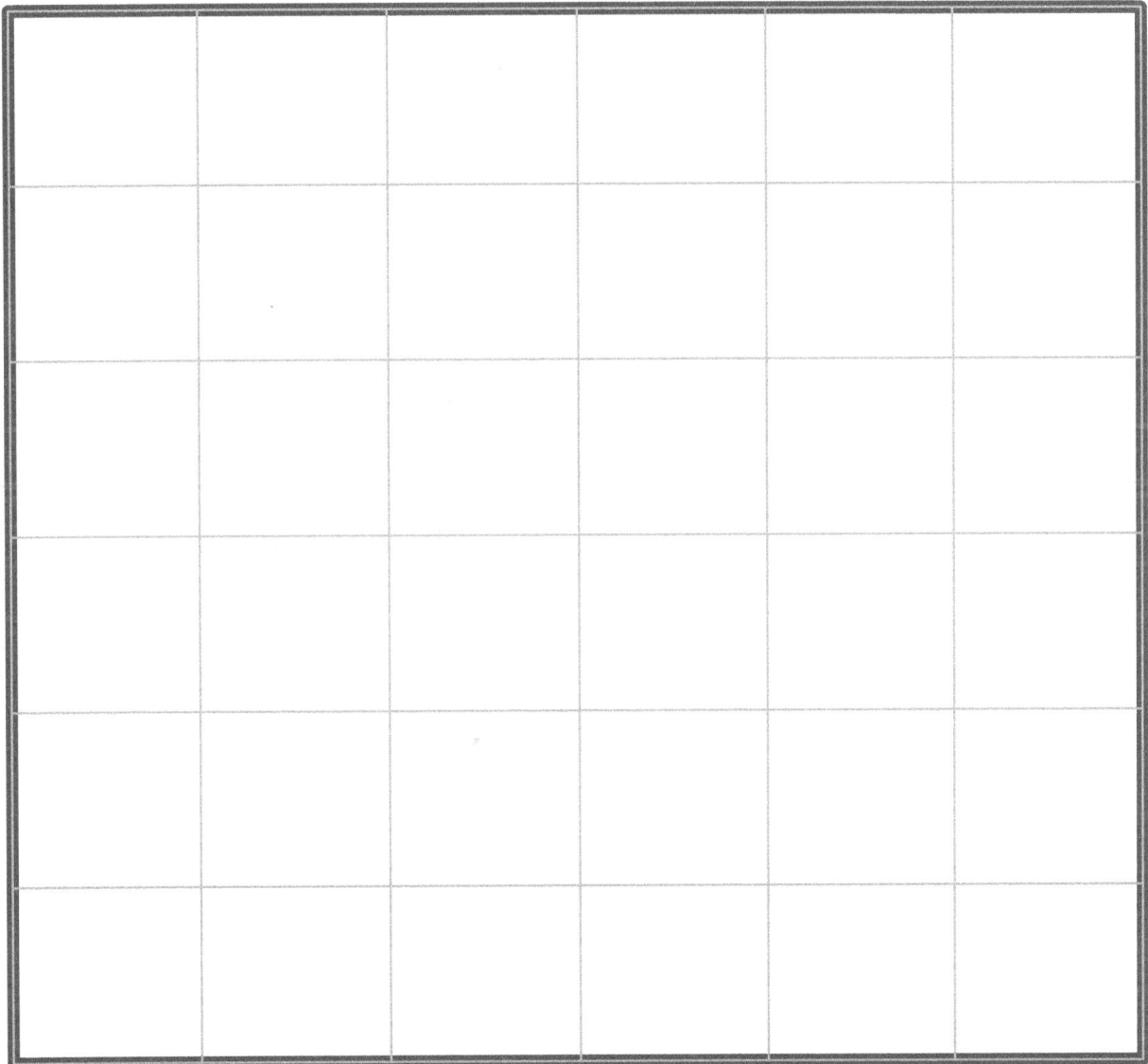

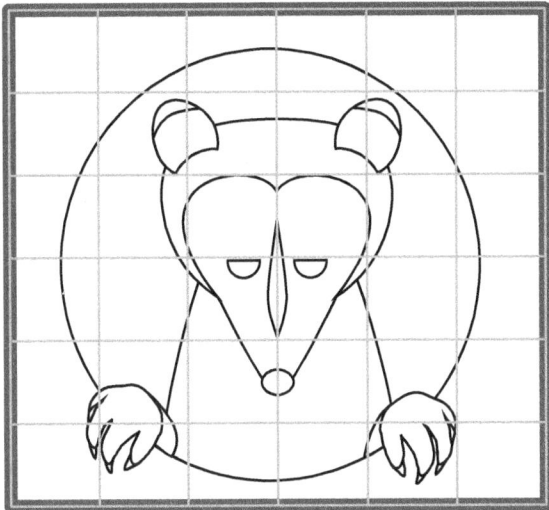

DRAW
THE
IMAGE

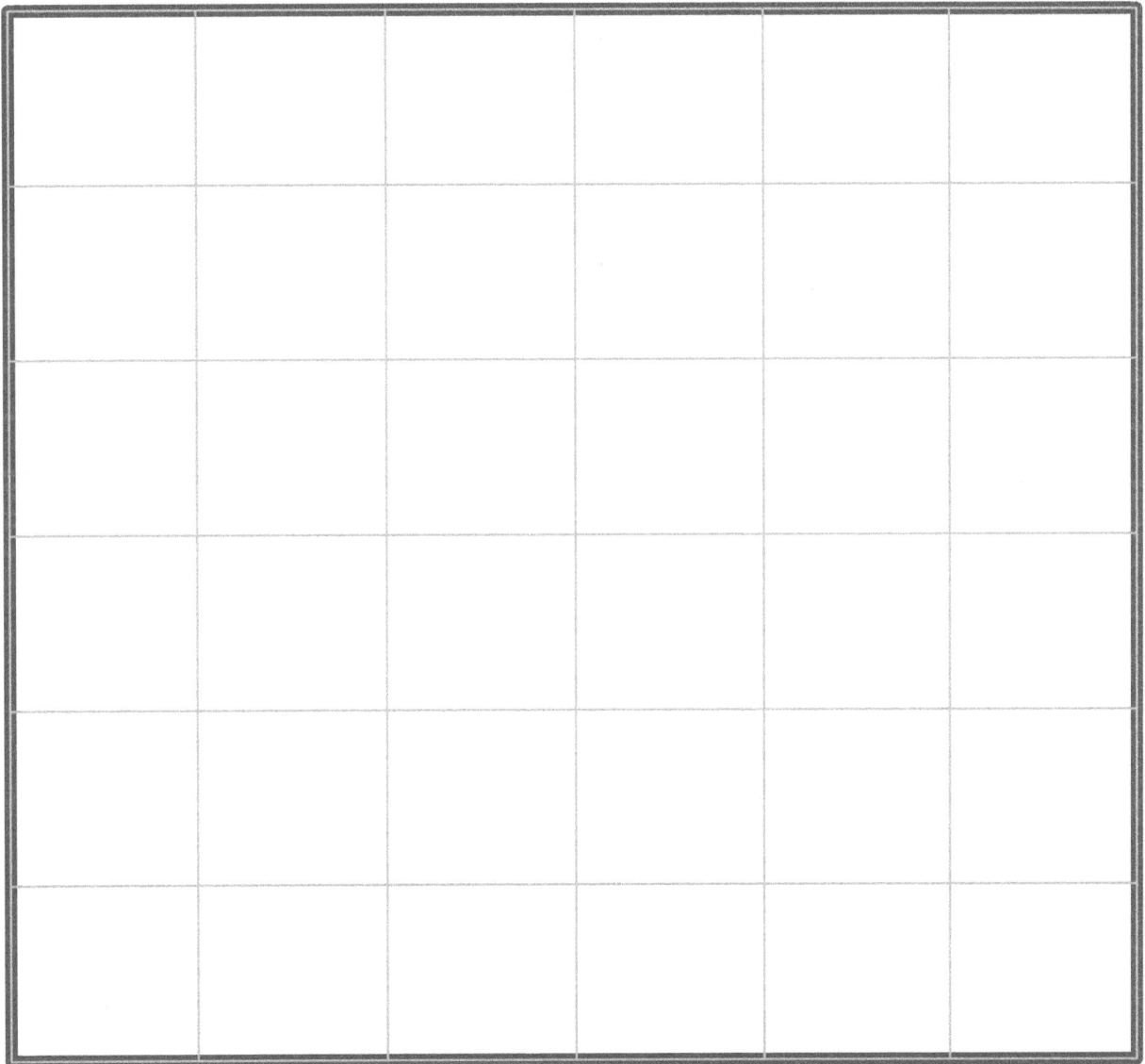

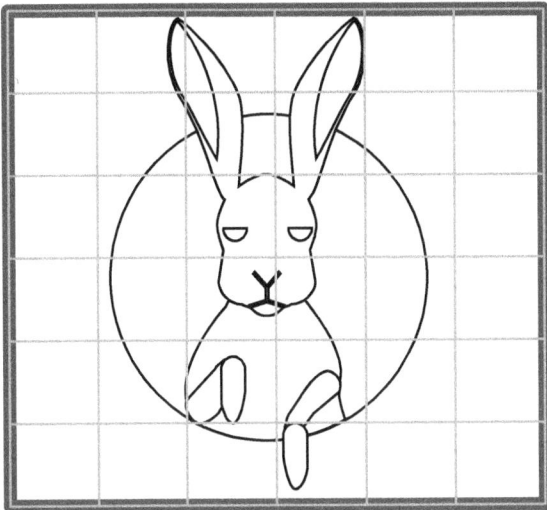

DRAW
THE
IMAGE

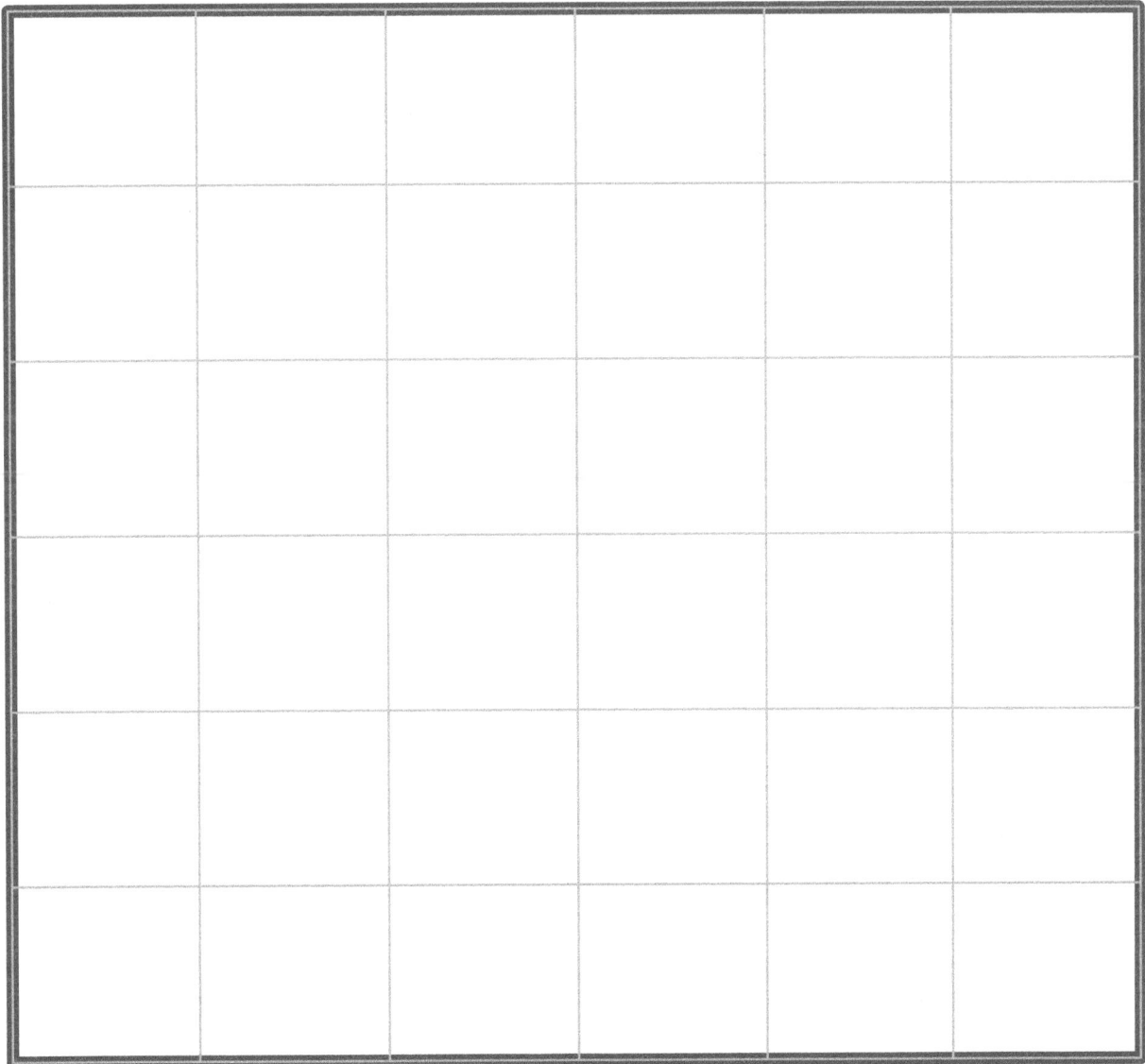

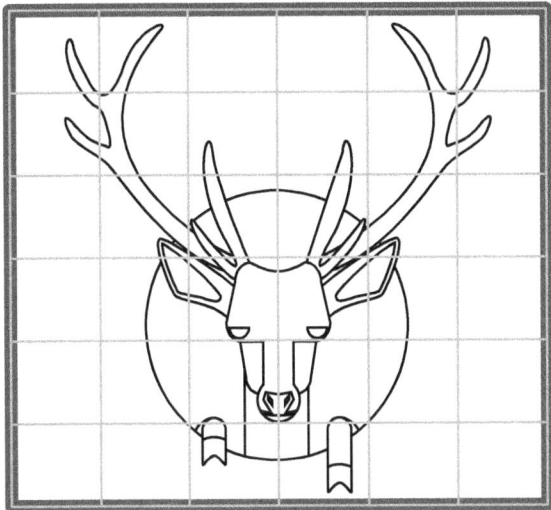

DRAW
THE
IMAGE

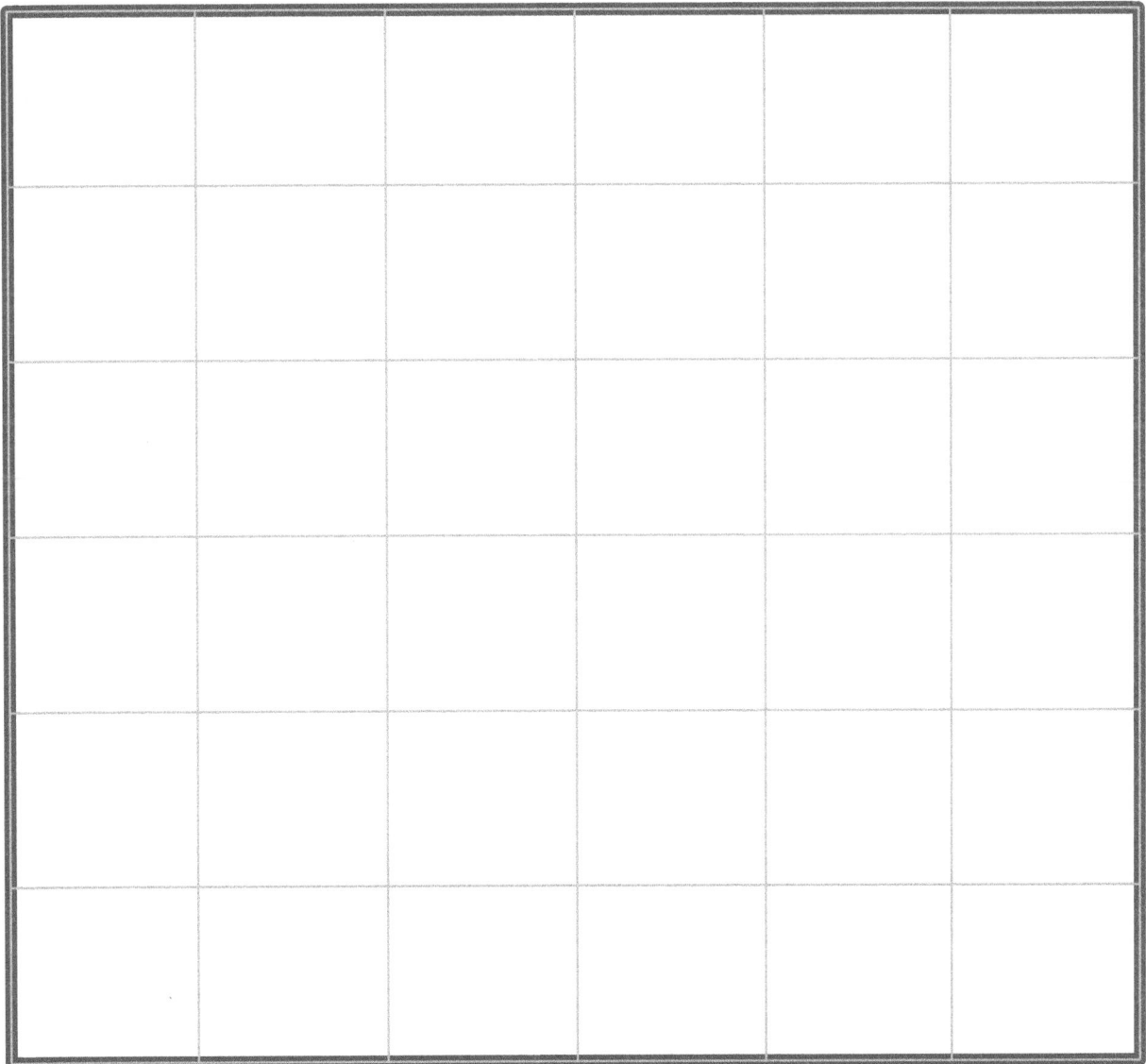

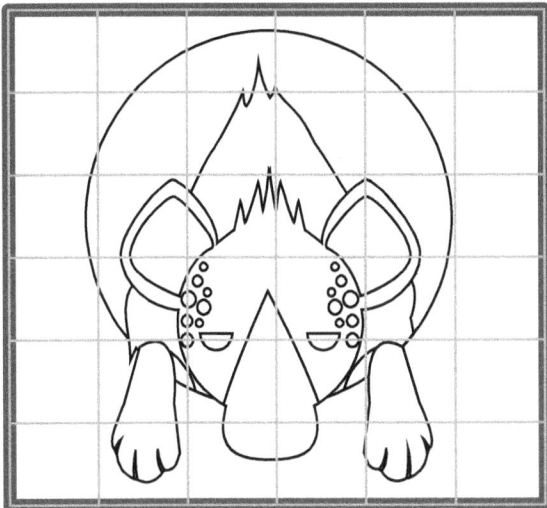

DRAW
THE
IMAGE

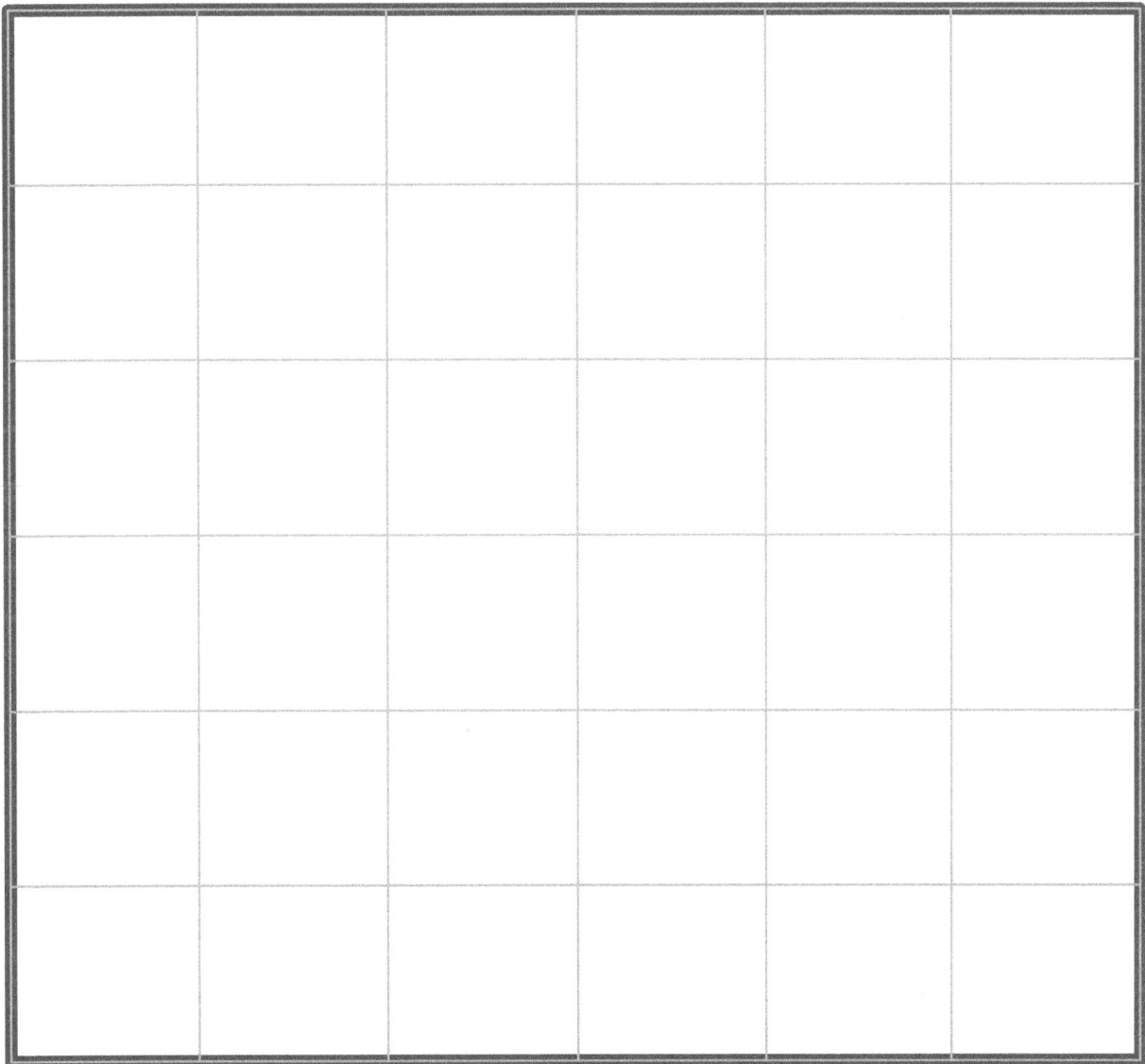

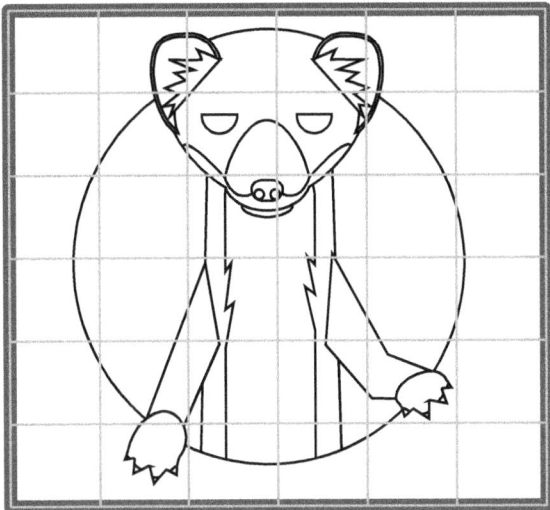

DRAW
THE
IMAGE

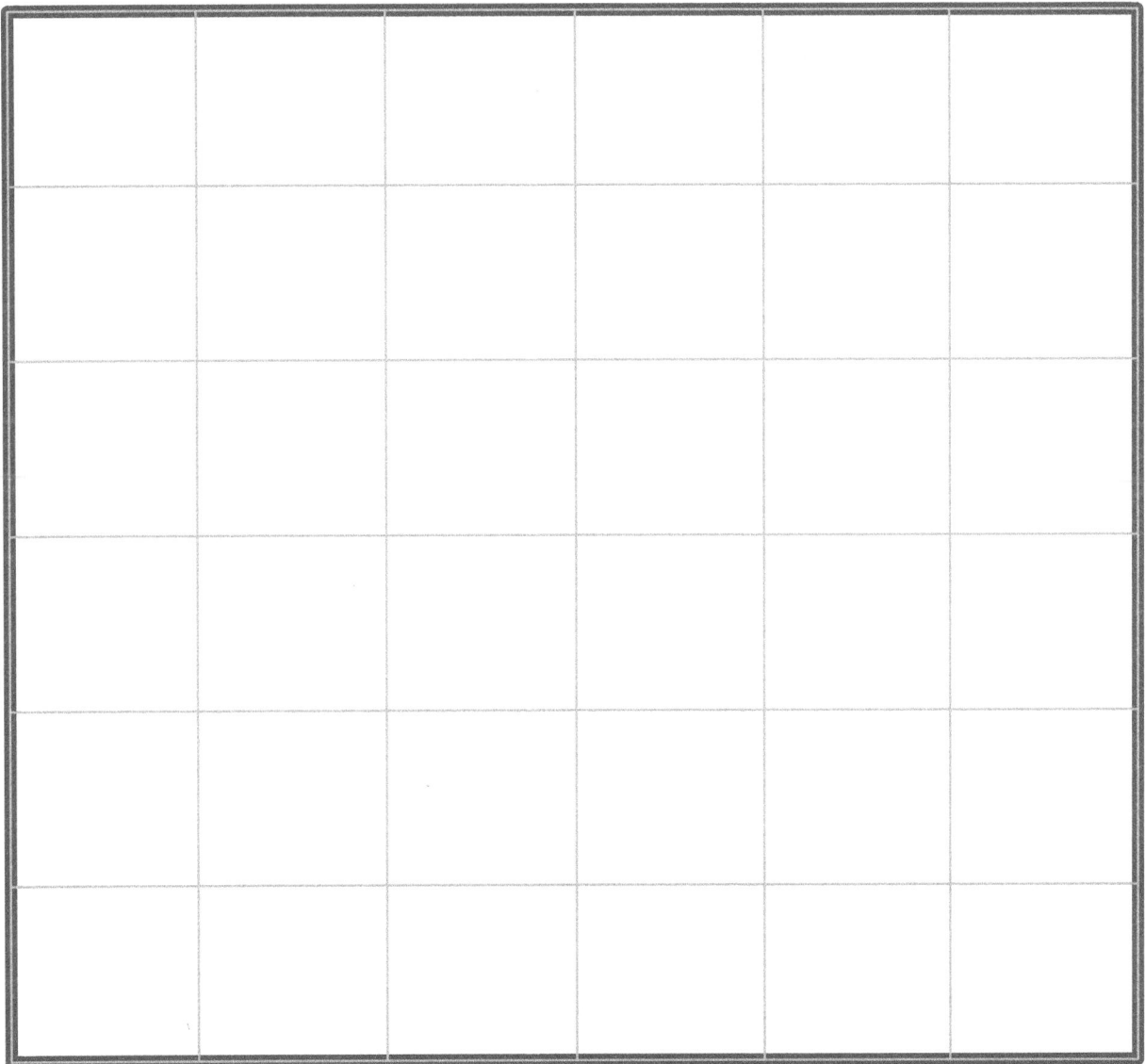

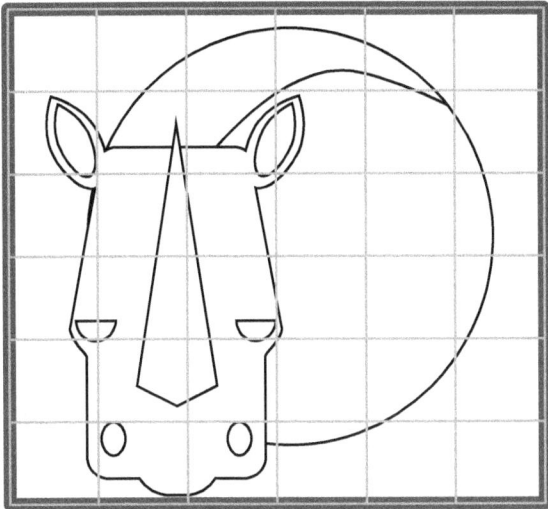

DRAW
THE
IMAGE

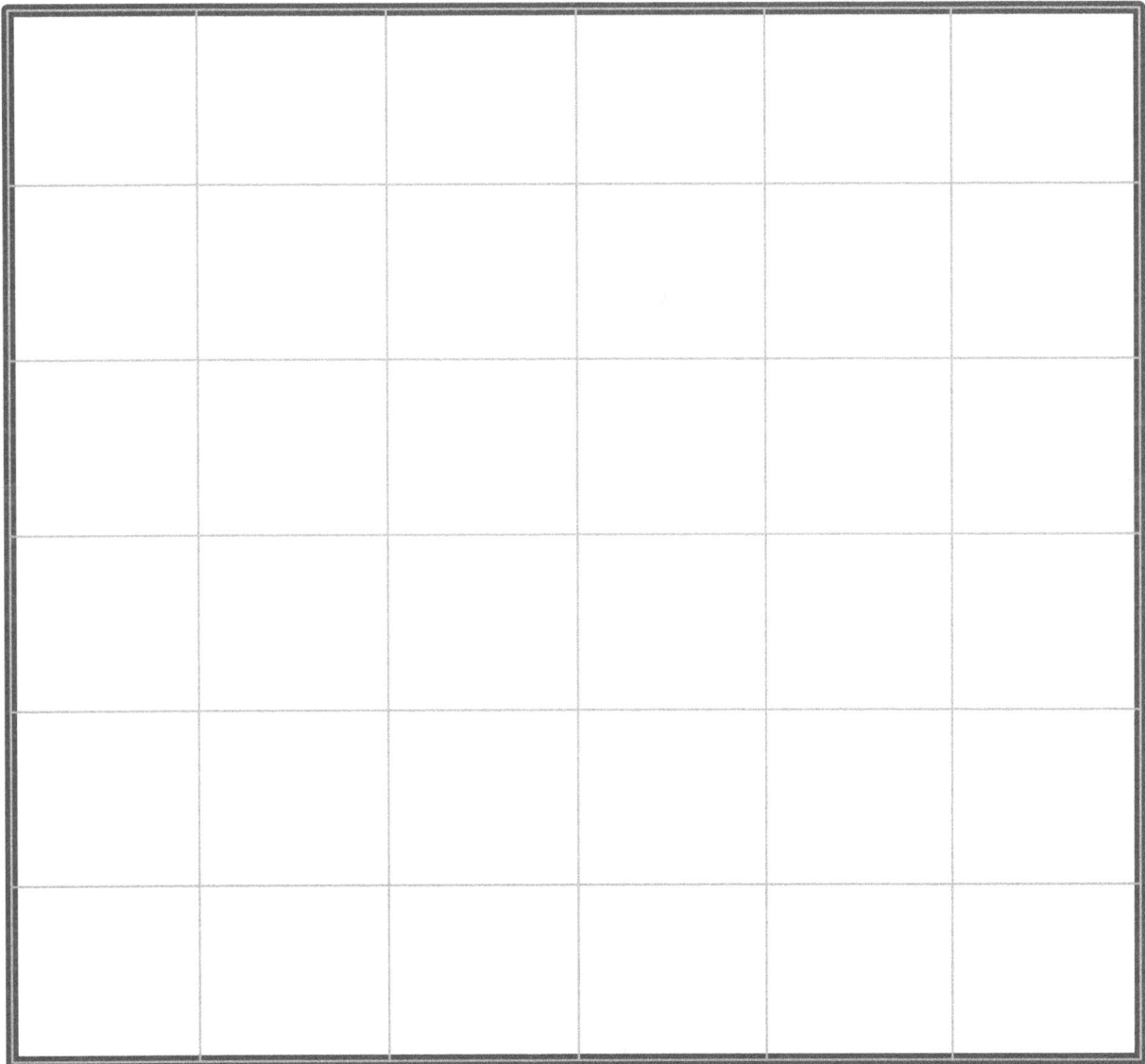

DRAW
THE
IMAGE

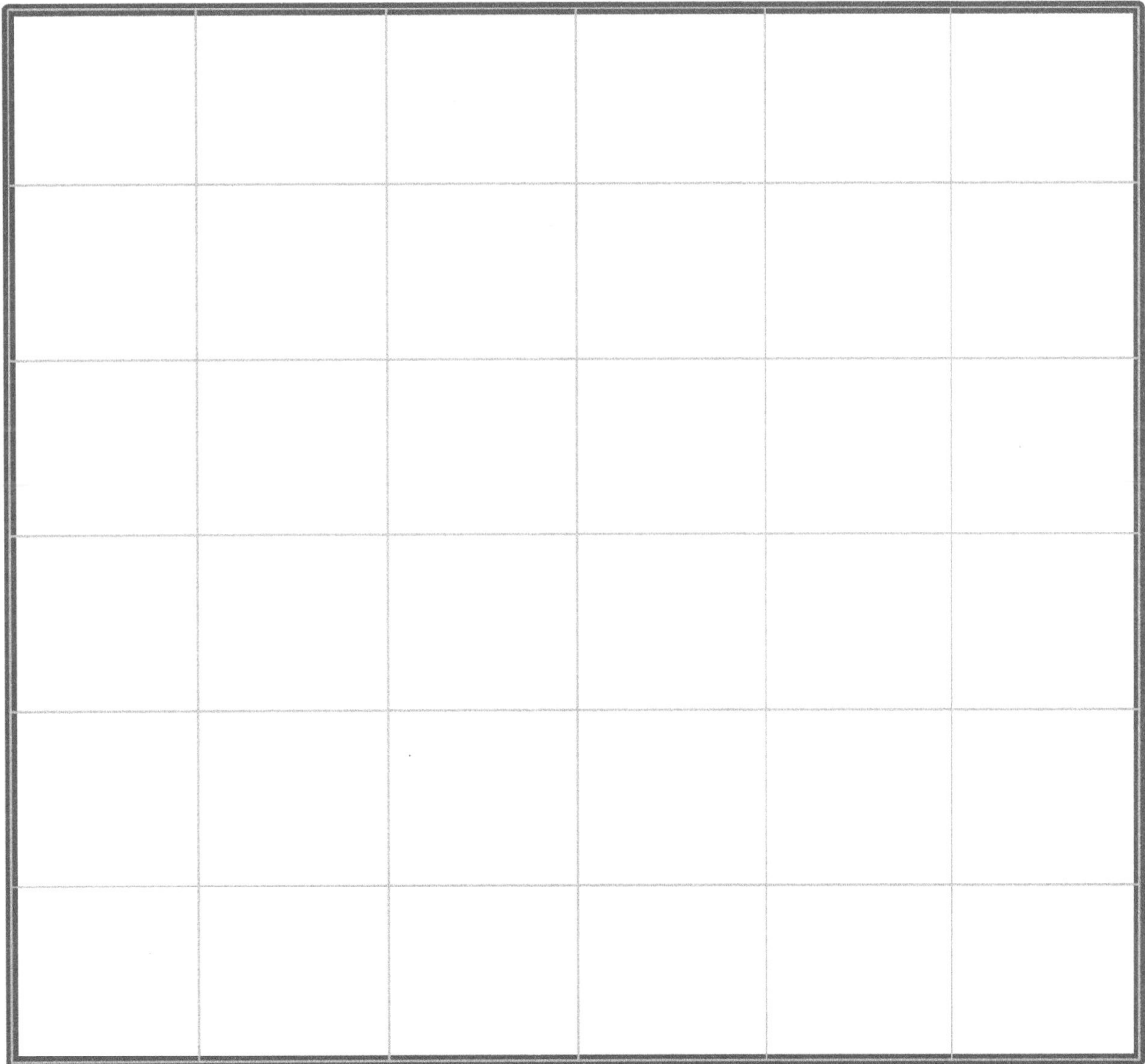

www.ingramcontent.com/pod-product-compliance
Lightning Source LLC
LaVergne TN
LVHW082323080426
835508LV00042B/1516